Tangled Twine

To find the single thread in a tangled maze of string takes patience, focus and persistence. The thread recovered can be woven into something useful or artistic. Our minds are tangled with a maze of experiences, observations, feelings and ideas. A moment of inspiration drops into that maze and it takes the same skills used on the string to find the simple, whole thread that becomes art.

Tangled Twine

John Camillo

David Lovell Publishing
Melbourne Australia

First published in 2016 by
David Lovell Publishing
PO Box 44, Kew East
Victoria 3102 Australia
tel/fax +61 3 9859 0000
publisher@davidlovellpublishing.com

© Copyright 2016 John Camillo
This work is copyright. Apart from any fair dealing for the purposes of private study, research, criticism or review, as permitted under the Copyright Act, no part may be reproduced by any process without written permission. Inquiries should be addressed to the publisher.

Design by David Lovell Publishing
Typeset in 12/16 Sabon
This edition printed by IngramSpark

National Library of Australia card number
and ISBN 978 186355 184 7

Full Catalogue-in-Publication details are available from the National Library of Australia

Excuses, excuses

It all had to wait because circumstances only now allow quiet mind time. So, here goes.

We are all exposed to inspirational moments that pounce on us, apparently from nowhere. I do not think they come from nowhere but that is how it seems when an event occurs. I wonder if it might just be true that those flashes we have, are generated in the waves of unseen but real energies that emanate from the ultimate source of life, light and everything else – the nearest star to us, our sun. Could it be that such waves of energy stimulate moments of inspiration and clarity about our existence, a bit like a cosmic dose of LSD? Heliophysics is still a young science and there are more questions than answers.

I listen with attention to interviews with song writers and poets and have often heard them deny credit for the inspiration they have experienced. 'I do not know where it came from', is something artists say. It could be feigned humility for the excellence they achieve but maybe not. It is possible that we all have the initial flash of an idea or picture or tune. The thing is that it takes concentrated effort to embody the magic of a moment into a finished, communicative product. There is truth in the old saying that good ideas are twopence

a ton. Most of them are not grabbed, moulded and polished into works of greatness.

It has been a most fortunate accident to have been part of a family brimming with stimulation in the most ordinary of ways. I stand in awe at the technical and artistic talents of my siblings, their ferocious self-confidence. This collection, however, is not about them though they make appearances. It is about my attempts at catching some of the moments that have flashed my mind. I offer them to you for what you might see.

These poems should be taken for what you might see in them. They do mean a lot to me and it is quite OK if that is where it stops. It is possible too that I may have botched the craft I have adopted, but there you are.

You will or will not find your own ways to deal with those flashes you surely experience. The special moments I have tried to grasp snared my attention between 2008 and 2016.

John Camillo September 2016

Contents

2008

Hello Cocky	3
They went there	5
Birdsville	9
Milparinka	11
Isabella, Charlie, Jet, Wynter	13

2009

Sydney	15
Egmont	17
Futility	19
New Plymouth	21
Coming home Aria	23
The great Up North	25
Enduring romance	27
Do not walk on acorns	29
Butterfly	31
What does it take?	33

2010

See gull	35
Clutter	37
Hope	39
Fernanda	41
Coolah	45
Burradoo	49
Armadale – The Dreamtime	53
Howlings	57

2011

Winter bloom	61
Always this way	63

2012

Eden	67
Cutta Cutta	69
The walk	71
Vigour	73
Spring	77
Homo Sapiens	79
Art, life and art	81

2013

Coolah	83
Tyra	87
Roadtrain driver	89
Blood on the wheels	91
Highways of lightning	93

2016

On the twelfth day	95
Queenstown	97
You	99

The Poems

Dandenong has always been on the edge of civilisation – not far from country. Nobody told the cockies or corellas or parrots or galahs that they should go. They have stayed. These beautifully wild, free birds often strafe our parks, gardens, electric wires, trapezing on fence wires, sliding down tin roofs, always noisy, often perched authoritatively atop our town hall spire. The sight of them is comical and tragic. The 'Leunig' I refer to is a renowned Australian romantic, pessimist cartoonist – not altogether unlike the cocky itself.

Tangled Twine

Hello Cocky

Broadcast cocky screech stifled in streetscape
Proud birds, gymnasts, flash through our trees
Balanced on light poles scrounging by drains
Cracking the day with their squawking

Where are the eucalypt stands, frost-bitten mornings to see
Where the ten mile creek beds, willows and hide logs free
Where the huge valleys that echo their calls
My Leunig heart soars, futile, feeling full for them.

Hello cocky, hello.

Pete and I were part of a convoy heading to Birdsville, the long way and across the Simpson. I was not happy at the time to take my ute across on that punishing drive. Next time I will. He and I headed home via the Birdsville track and down through the Adelaide Hills back to Victoria. For those days when we were in the convoy, the group adjusted well to the dynamics. It was a great trip.

They went there

For Matt and Albi, Denny and Kerry, Karen and Jim and Ails and PK and Tony and Lorraine and Dicko and Louise and my good mate Pete

City folk in fact you are
But that skin falls tonight
With your trucks and utes and tents and boots
Step aboard for a magical flight

Forget for a time the things that you do
You are mine now give me your hands
I will show you and get to know you
Just who and what you are

I will chill you to your creaky bones
You will thirst like never before
And one day soon you will rise to love
The feelings you've come to me for

You will sit for hours along the track
Before you begin to know
I'm not a place without a face
But a place to face what is in you

You cannot reach me, know me or teach me
At best you'll get to glimpse

Tangled Twine

Your camera's blink and you might think
You've caught me unaware

But is it all about what you see
Is that all I can mean
No, you see, I see inside you
You cannot hide out here

When you gasp at the star-shot night sky
And stare at infinity
It is not just another snapshot
To look at over tea

Look at me, damn it, look real close
Before you retire to your tent
Infinity pulls at your smallness
Carries you into deep space

And when you stand with your back to the fire
Coffee in chilled hands
Her eyes reflecting the day-born horizon
Does miracle leap to mind

Do you turn to your partner
And hold your hands
Do your hearts meet in that place
Because that is what you are here for

I'm not just a pretty face.

First light of day on the edge of the Simpson Desert, standing atop Big Red. We are a long way from city lights. The night had been deeply dark once the fire dropped and the only light came from the Milky Way. Morning, making the fire is the first job after taking the shovel for a walk and it is the aroma of a fresh brew that brings everybody to the one spot. It was a moment.

Birdsville

How still the desert morning
How chill, moist, the dawn air sits
Camp fire crackle brew stirs the sleepers
From black heavy tent night press

They sip a promise from black billy tea
The night show brilliance closes
Attention drops to the dune tops' orange
Sleep crusted eyes, stiffened hair forgotten

Ten figures back from black they turn
To catch the horizon warming
And unsure if the things they'd seen
Were real or just a dreaming.

It was a thriving outback town when the mines were working. But it has been a while since then. Tourist buses still call in and the pub is still open. For all of the place's solitude it is impressive. The few locals alone are worth the visit.

Milparinka

Milparinka gold all gone
Friendly folk, Southwark Cold
Secret yabbies Michael brings in
Dry creek, crab pots, someone's lying
Outback humour, laughing, crying

Sit still, listen, wind howls through
Travellers stop and locals mix
Milparinka
Mick's gone fishing, Donald's shooting roos

Men build the line, roads, tracks and mines
Energy bursting stations thrive
But it … just waits, it does not care
It's bigger, stronger, always there
It … takes its time, time's in hand.

As happens with so many of us, we became grandparents. We have all the predictable emotions concerning the four of them. This poem is a suggestion that there is something to learn from the clarity of their vision before the inevitable corruption takes root in their lives and they end up being just as flawed as we are.

Isabella, Charlie, Jet, Wynter

You are with us you give us
A chance to get right
To see with clear eyes
Chisel plaque off our lives
To reach for embrace
Nestle without fear
To listen and wonder
Dream, play, imagine
And always be near

Laughing and crying with gusto
Lost in a world of your making
All we can do is watch you and rue
What we've lost what you've got
Try to walk in your shoes
Holding your hands while you guide us
Bring colour back to our eyes.

Of course, the subject could be much more broadly dealt with than I have done here. We were staying with our son and his wife who were living in Dulwich Hill. I walked the streets there and in Newtown. We also took the train to Circular Quay, met our son for coffee in one of the many little nooks where the coffee addicts find their favourite hit. Sydney, as you know, has flavours that are unique. It has always been a great place to visit.

Sydney

Coffee pockets, pick a place
Caffeine fuels the pace
Barista is so sacred here
Artwork in the fluff

Bitumen and concrete patchwork
Bulging, chipped and cracked
The roads are stuffed they know it's thus
They let you in, make little fuss

Inner urban millionaires
Grow veggies out the front
The houses have despaired, they sag
They hold one another up

She picks at weeds in every crack
He patches up the render
Been here since '55
Owe nothing to the lender

Their son has picked a retirement home
He wants them to be safe
They want to go, he prays they do
He'd sell it all, his great escape

And life goes on in Sydney
All motion, no complaints
Life to live, a wave to catch
A toll to pay, a deal to snatch.

It stands above the landscape, dominates it, not least of all by driving the weather. It offers an eerie sight on a winter evening when New Plymouth is already dark and the last of the sun catches the snow-peaked mountain. It is breath taking. I lived for a year in its shadow and under its spell. Dan is a good friend I met in our teacher training years in Sydney. He is from New Plymouth and is now back there.

Egmont

Skin-peeling wind sleet ices through the fields
Like it has done since the mountain was formed
Since it first sucked the cloud banks around it
And spat with incredible force

It sucks at the people who live there
And never lets them go
Controls every life in the living
And never lets them know

When it called him Dan came home
A salmon fighting upstream
He came to the place of his spawning
His mountain would set his heart free.

He picked up at the school where he left it
But stayed outside its walls
He mows the grass, replaces glass
Disposes all the rubbish

The youngsters brush past him, do not see him
Their eyes on distant goals
They'll grow, then go, like he did
Till Egmont calls them home

Have you ever had
the sense that you move outside the
bubble of what others think is real?
I had the experience while visiting
the school where I taught in the very
first year of a career. It had been forty
years and in spite of the claims that the
school was state of the art, I could see
little change at all. My observations
were not welcome.

Futility

Poets and troubadors write in black ink
Their inspiration flashes
It fades against indifference
I wonder what the point is

The corridors and classrooms are just like '66
Desks all in line, a platform, a blackboard up the front
Frozen thought, suspended evolution
What on earth have they been doing

He's got an Aussie accent
Be careful what you say
Be sure to condescend him
He'll soon be gone away, aye.

Caught between Mount Egmont (Taranaki) and the ocean, this is one beautiful place. Weather is dominant, sometimes extreme. The people just go about their business seemingly unflustered by the Antarctic blasts or the crashing seas.

New Plymouth

Grassy knolls across the walkway
Boulders hold back the sea
Egmont, enigma, stands on the left
The Tasman heaves on the right

Chill factor zero screams off the snow
Slashes at farmlands, no quarter shown
It wheels through the outskirts, right into town
Snagged by the high rise, down every lane

It pounces pedestrians, they never complain
Jackets and hoodies, sunglasses and scarves
Three quarter shorts, just how do you grasp
New Zealand's a paradox, don't even ask.

There is always something miraculous about the comfort of modern flight. It is bizarre when you think that you are travelling at 1000 kph at 37,000 ft, sipping coffee or taking in a movie. My mind was still on the things I had seen in New Zealand and at the same time this music grabbed my attention. But then, Sarah Brightman does that for you.

Coming home Aria

Night flight, locked inside the kite
A movie, a meal, BO and beer
Headphone classics, curved cabin light
Genuine attention from stewards in flight

Two hours to Tulla, 'Pearl Fisher's' duet
Crashes Egmont's cliffs, I can see it
Avalanche opera ripping the slopes
Baritone thunder splitting the ice
And an angel's voice breathing the mist.

Some places have the power to overwhelm. There is much of that going on all over the outback. Jim Jim is a good drive from the Crocodile resort and a challenging walk once you get there. But it is worth the effort to struggle over the boulders, deep into the canyon, eyes fixed on the perilous stacks of rock slabs until you get to the swimming hole, deep, chilled and quiet.

The great Up North

Jim Jim Falls is hard to get to
Follow close, watch your step, feel your way
Towering, leaning, crumbling gorge
A drink water or die sort of day

The pool, a jewel, a prize to hold
And walkers to swimmers, crablike crawl
Rocks, boulders fallen heavy
Can't stop the plunge, the chilling fall

Fractured rock face threatens
Sandstone rickety chip stacks lean
Fear subdued by awe, they scramble
Trusting time is with them before the chip stacks fall.

Tangled Twine

I guess that many of our experiences within relationships are common. We strive to hold ourselves together especially when we face those uncomfortable times of doubt about what we are doing. The road is strewn with wreckage, I know, but I offer this thought for what it might be worth at critical moments. The key has something to do with reflecting rather than reacting.

Enduring romance

Scorched in a blast of indifference?
Don't know where to turn?
Pick up a good book
Walk the dog
Tomorrow will be different!

Our species is born of the star nearest us. We yearn to explore the solar system and ultimately the rest of the cosmos. For all of our searching for enlightenment across the planet, to the moon, Mars and beyond, it is possible to get a result much closer to home. Children, like acorns, are packed with potential. We crush acorns under our feet and ruin the children. How smart is that? Our doom is genetically coded.

Do not walk on acorns

Star lit life force
Creeping out, reaching
Generations burned out
What's worth keeping

Inspiration, mind aloft
Comets in our minds
Crash through carry off
Things to find

Where will they take you, galactic far
Beyond eyes' reach and back to your feet
Blue sky blindness, earthbound fear
Too far out there, but it's all in here

Legions of mysteries beyond the moon
We yearn to probe for meaning
Oblivious, it seems, to the end of our noses
Under which wisdom is sleeping

Locked in an acorn a mighty tree
Held in a child's hand easy
Too many crushed beneath our feet
Too many children weeping.

I watched the style of a lollipop man supervising a pedestrian crossing near two local schools. He would high five different children and march theatrically on and off the crossing. He did a great job. But some would look at him with suspicion, such is the fear that exists about the dangers to children. It is possible, of course, that he could have evil intent. He knows the risks he takes but believes it is better to see the joy on young faces at the interaction than to allow fear to rule his behaviour.

Butterfly

Fingertip taste touch glorious to feel
Full bodied innocence reaching
So easy to spoil, so fragile a thing
Stand back, watch it unfurl

What is a child but a gleam in the eye
Of the crusty old man in the fading
A memory raised and savoured again
There is hope he thinks passing by

She throws a look over her shoulder
At the man she sees every day
He always appears to be happy
Always stops for 'g'day'

But his innocence got lost in the darkness
Like the butterfly catcher net poised
One wrong word and her wings would collapse
Trapped, enfolded and spoiled

There is hope for the species
She skips on her way
There's a smile all over her soul
She glides in the sun of the morning
Oblivious, untainted and whole.

This is the old story of the individual search for meaning outside of the requirements of the flock. It raises the question of the need we have for affirmation. Does it matter if nobody sees?

What does it take?

The seagull on the flagpole
Sits easy, without friends
Still it is, aloft, alone
And wonders
Whatever a seagull wonders

I am small, it thinks
Nothing at all in the scheme of things
I watch and I learn and take things in
Today I did a pirouette
Did anybody see?

Another look at the same idea as the previous poem – looking at the same bird on the same flagpole on top of the town hall in New Plymouth. 'Jonathan Livingstone Seagull' was a delightful story parading as a child's book. It was a while ago and it stirred a few minds.

See gull

He sits as a bird sits
Standing
Atop a flagpole, silent
A misty eve below

He does not see it
He stares ahead, afar
And follows the spent day
Sink into the Tasman Sea

The flock's long gone
Jonathan, outcast, stands alone
And wonders still
What it would take to break even.

Take a walk through a Trash'n'Treasure market, anywhere. You will paw over items that have stories that nobody will tell. It is a short leap to look at the way old people are regarded. They too are chock full of stories, many of them instructive, but nobody has the time or inclination to listen. Life could be easier if they just went away.

Clutter

Old wagon wheel behind the shed
Split timber spokes and rusted rim
Photos sepia, forgotten folk
World War One suit, a wedding coat

Grandma's jewellery, biscuit tins
Briar pipes, old safety pins
No obituaries for all these things
Chock full of stories locked within

Helmets, hall stands, scales and vases
Paintings, worn out chairs, fat arses
Enid Blyton Dr Seuss books
Stuff that gets no second looks

Take heed old man, old lady too
No more work, nothing to do
Collectors are circling, examining you
How much will you bring?

Is that your total worth?
Your wisdom counts for naught?
Your stories rattle on, no one listening here
You clearly have no purpose

Please leave now, Oh … sweet repose.

The old tree launches a young bird on its first flight. Is there a metaphor here for our continued value to the world, even if, like the tree, we are but a shadow of our former flourishing selves?

Hope

A tree should have a canopy
Broad reach, deep roots and life support
For birds and spiders, bugs, cicadas
Living off its bounty

But this old one cannot do that
It barely holds its feet
Stripped of bark, its limbs all gone
Sad, standing skeleton, and yet a sacred tree

Its barren grey crusty top this morning
Caught the early light
And from its hollowed trunk there hopped
A young galah all trimmed for its first flight

It leapt fearless into the morning, falling, falling
Then triumphantly gliding
And landed clumsily, relieved and amazed.
So was I.

A one-time visitor within the family is a talented artist, one from a distinguished line. She drew an image of a little girl I came to know and happily continue to. Looking at the charcoal sketch it all passed before my mind. It is a good thing.

Fernanda

A baby girl, year old at most
Crochet dress, a ribbon tie
Motionless sitting, charcoal drawn
A future locked within

The eyes, wells, dark pools, alert
Looking straight ahead
She does not see beyond the frame
Caught in '51

Her mother dressed her for the portrait
That is clear to see
Soft buttoned shoes, short socks, brushed locks
An expectation in the air

Sixty years, I see her still
Broad forehead curly hair
The eyes still look straight ahead
The full lips tell a story

She grew to fullness, stretched her limbs
Met the world head on
A family of her own now grown
Her blessings on their heads

Her threesome look at what she is
They thrived beneath her wings
She guided, chided, stood beside them
Through everything they did

Partner, mother, teacher, lover
Who knows her knows to love her
As those who loved that little tot
All those years ago.

It happened on a long road trip that I pulled into the tiny town of Coolah in central northern NSW. I had noticed the derelict shack just out of town and when I stood before the cenotaph and read the names it all became something special. The names on the monument included eight pairs of brothers, four threesomes, two fours and a list of five bearing the same names. These were the sons of local farming families and they went to war, never to return. One can only imagine the grief through the district. The cost of patriotism was too high for those families.

Cooolah

A house, all leaning, broken, bared, alone
Sliding out of time, its time long passed
A shell, a fossil, paddock-bound and still
The only hint of life the morning chill
Breath of the ghosts of Coolah

Grey mist spoons the cenotaph
An old farmer reads the names
He shivers, not from cold, and weeps
Brothers, friends and kin, all gone
Coolah sent its sons for keeps

A humming rises in the old man's chest
His sadness turns to pride
The baker and mechanic hear it
Cross the street, join in

He lifts his eyes, his throat still hums
It turns into a roar
The town locks arms, walks behind
You could hear their voices sing

'Too many sons slaughtered, Coolah
Too many gone to war
Uncles, brothers never seen more
Only photos came home

'Too many sons slaughtered, Coolah
Too many gone to war
Sons of Australia taken, fallen
Too much pain for all

'NO MORE'

It was a fascinating adventure to be recruited by a religious order and to find myself in a Junior Novitiate. It was a boarding school where 14 to 17-year-old aspirants would complete secondary studies before the heavy work of the novitiate and then teacher training. It was a seven year stint. If you have ever watched the whole of the movie, 'The Nun's Story', you will have some idea of how intense the experience can be.

Burradoo

Swim time mist, everything a dream
Daybreak frost walk, three miles to town
Woollen gloves, frozen hair, hurry, chapel bound
Teeth chatter no matter, God to be found

A country lane, a railway line
A tiny railway station
A fog that clings to everything
Our highland winter's winding

Frost-bitten tap drips, no drink here
Snap frozen paddocks ice crystal morn
Hurried striding, sliding, ice bits flying
Race on first to warm

A gravel driveway, big old gate
Pine trees line the path
Sentinels that pierce the mist
Some standing bare some lightning split

Cones, toadstools scattered there
Pine needles blanket thick
We kick them, throw them, scamper home
For a steaming country breakfast

Once stables, now our classrooms wait
The dew drips off the glass
Iced puddles, red brick courtyard
Are first to catch the sun

And we are warm now, fattened
Eager for our books
We skid and slide and giggle here
Believing life's all good

To Mick and Pete and Dennis too
Paul, John and Ron and Peter Pat
Pete Broman, Bushie Neville
Bill Fanning, David and Mick Mac
Jim Fabris shone a tenor strong, Joe ran like the wind
McCabe brushed off the heavy stuff like ducks do to water
We all did what we had to do
Lambs led to the slaughter.

We are, of course, a link in a very long genetic chain. The thing is that we are often blinded by the arrogant delusion of individualism. Look at some of your old photos and you will see striking resemblances between those of your generation and those who preceded. Is the cloning just physical? You have to work that out.

Armadale – The Dreamtime

It reaches out and grabs the mind it does
It struggles to connect, today is such a reach
But chromosomic threads, they weave through time
And out pops poppa, grandma too
Everyone returns.

Take heed young ones, you burst with youth
But you have been about before
Have you learned, improved or even known?
Your slate is scored before you saw
No one thought to warn

The restlessness you feel
Your father felt
His mother before him
She wept her life for being nought
And futile routine fraught

She fought and dragged her young uns
Placed them on their path
Her mother fought and lost, and left
Her children scattered, fostered strewn
She could not know how many times around

And what of the men and burdens borne?
Their seed washed in the fertile stream
And time through time it sprouts anew
I see it in my grandchild's eyes
And hear it in my daughters' cries

They knew to work and carried risk
Depression tested, chances wasted
Seized the day that offered little
Reaped the whirlwind where they stood
And did the best they could

Who am I now, who sits here writing
Mother's father's, father's seed
Who strives to make a mark in me
To make up for before?

The theme from the previous offering is pursued here. It is an attempt to understand my place as a link in a very long chain of generations. I was on the train from Dandenong to the city of Melbourne and had to pass through the suburbs of my childhood. Many of our adventures were along the train line between Malvern and Toorak, especially the now missing briquette sheds at Malvern. The 'New Malvern' was one of four picture theatres in the suburb. Saturday matinees were popular with kids at that time.

Howlings

From the train I saw where they'd stood and I heard
Howlings of ghosts that stirred
'Briquette sheds where you played', screamed the howling
From the squeezed wheel squealing beneath me

'The "New Malvern" and spears from the wood mill
Your friends and your brothers in arms
Warring raggedy children
Your brothers tagging along

'You rolled billy carts on the Armadale ramps
Pursued by the station man's scolding
And your clattering, giggling mischief
Sends echoes through the tunnels of time'

Then through the bridge under High Street
The howlings peaked in my head
Ma Annie's there still near the corner
Pa tapping and smoking his pipe

A little girl cries on the footpath
Her father is calling her in
Face pressed to the glass, I'm transfixed and ask
Just where is this train coming from

Then in the hearing the mind starts clearing
Their job is not done yet at all
They are here somewhere inside me
I can hear them rattling my bones

There is more to living than being
Their being here's linked to a line
Existence entwined, unravelling time
Giving birth – the warp of creating

'Connect, you fool, how long must it take
To widen your being, get to the meaning
Get close to where you stand'
I am flashed in that moment, don't know if I can

'You can, you can. It's easy to do
Do nothing but call to your children.
Call all your days till they hear you
Long after you seem to have gone

'This is the work of creation you do
In the end its no trick don't be taken
And not one thing more is needed from you
Than to have a hand in the making.'

How do we get the best out of a long term relationship? I would not dare to theorise too much on this, on what could be a volatile subject. Having said that, it is possible to appreciate the dance we do around each other and see that dance as romance in itself. The idea of 'romance' is not a narrow one.

Winter bloom

Mist wet, grey morning
Cradled behind her warmth
I watch the tangle of magnolia
Clawing at the window
Its dripping tendrils alive with buds
That promise winter bloom

Our toes press familiar, together.
We lie there doona wrapped,
Still, mixing morning breath.
My right hand reaches, cupping.
She moves a little feigning sleepy
Wary, knowing what comes next, and asks

'Could I have a cup of tea?'

We live in troubled times with collapsing economies, persistent outbreaks of war, droughts and floods, hurricanes, typhoons and bush fires. There are mass shootings of innocents, shattering of families, outrageous levels of drug use, both prescribed and illegal. Tens of millions of refugees are on the move and our over-crowded nations are environmentally toxic. A growing number of species, both fauna and flora, teeter on the edge of extinction. Political systems show a vacuum of leadership and an unhealthy penchant for corruption. How does one find a way through all of this? I do not know. Greater awareness, though, cannot be a bad thing.

Always this way

Rain falls summer
The birds are breeding
Dams are full, it's been a while
A decade long

Dusted dreams awaken
Germinate the ground
And life goes on in cycles
Inevitably around

It seems the drought has shifted
World governments are flaming
Streets awash with protest
Obese oppress the starving

Bankers hog the harvest
Their noses in the trough
The holocaust consumption
Has turned upon itself

You cannot grow forever
Self-evidence ignored
The beast full grown now salivates
Its appetite a plague

And fires outrun the checking
Destruction's all that's seen
Collapsing empires falling, reeling
Embers fanned by greed

But fire's a purifier
Self-interest turns to ash
And the wheeling of time round the circle
Starts it all afresh

The south-east coast of NSW is a great place for paradise. They call the place Eden. The town has a rich history in killing whales, netting huge hauls of fish and chopping down trees to supply woodchip for Japanese interests. Right now the whaling has been confined to the museum, there are few trawlers making money and the world has turned against forestry that takes old trees. Eden is in crisis. On the other hand it is a fantastic place to take in bush walks, coastal activities and the whale watching. In spite of that effort I see Eden as a sad place.

Eden

'Australasia' pub, bar, TAB and fight zone
Where the whalers and the axemen stood
Shared their triumphs and their woes
Where sweat wet sinewed arms were raised
The weak cheered on the strong

'Time please gents', 100 years, time all spent
The auctioneer rings the bell
And like an old boxer, rusted limbs, spread-eagled nose
His eyes a dusty blue
The pub signs off a lifetime, reluctantly it's true

Timber bleedin' fish feeding Eden
A co-op, a cannery, a fishermen's wharf
It clings to the rocks and Twofold Bay
Determined it won't fall off

In the fighter's head all his bouts play out
Shadows weaving all around
A feint, a driving clinch, a jab
His restless feet reel but hold
No way he's going down

He doesn't know the crowd's all gone
No stomach for the sight.

Just south of Katherine in the Northern Territory you will find a set of limestone caves. There are tours every hour, managed by local Indigenous rangers. The claustrophobic atmosphere evaporates when they turn on the lights. I visited the place twice, three years apart.

Cutta Cutta

Cutta Cutta shining caves
They stop the mind with awe
Hidden lights fall across the folds
The drips, the spires, the moulded bulge

This is the weeping earth
Ten thousand years a tear.

(2009)

Cutta Cutta here we are
Three years gone
You've grown one tenth a millimetre
And I've not grown that much

Moulded, folded, glittered earth you are
You draw us near to you
Propped, transfixed, our can't touch reaching reaches you
And your embrace is a waiting thing
A patient, certain thing.

(2012)

Do *we force feed our children the deeds of other times, or do we not? There should be confidence that the understandable indifference of young people will become something else when their youth gives way to other great mindsets.*

The walk

Don't box up the trophies
Leave the photos on the wall
Best and fairest, ribbons blue
Long distance racer, swimming champ

And here along the passageway
A gold-framed Arts degree
Underneath, a uniform, weapon at his side
A striking pose, familiar nose, unfamiliar clothes

What echoes sound, what things were done
What meaning to it all
A few mementos for a while
Just footprints, moving sand

Don't box up the trophies
Leave the photos on the wall
Let the children see and ponder
Before the pictures fall

A profile, a certain look, a gesture
Just little things that linger, jump the gap
So they might learn before they go
They have not stood alone.

Tangled Twine

There are surely many ways to ask a question. Maybe this one is bizarre but I kind of like the idea that, no matter how energetic a life might be, it stops and it stops for good. Why do we bother? Our behaviour indicates that we have either answered the question to our satisfaction or that we just have not bothered to ask it.

Vigour

The lights come on, vigour blinks, vigour stirs

Vigour, vigour, vigour, vigour
Vigour his and hers

Vigour wailing, vigour crawling, suckling and talking
Vigour run, vigour float, vigour rocking the boats.
Vigour, vigour, vigour, vigour
Sucking life in gulps

Vigour, vigour, vigour, vigour
Vigour, vigorous

Vigour drive, vigour read, vigour build, vigour breed
Vigour cope, vigour thrive, vigorous
Vigour save no time, vigour you're alive
Full of vigour, happy vigour, bugger everything else

Vigour work, vigour spend, vigour save what you can
Keep your eye on the ball, vigour wise, grow tall
Vigour climb the tree, vigour one, two, three
Use your vigour with all rigour, get in now, get it all

Vigour, vigour, vigour, vigour
Vigour, vigorous

Then vigour crisis, vigour trip, vigour tumble, vigour fall
Vigour dodge, vigour lie, vigour hit the wall
Vigour stand so still, try to listen, vigour call
Vigour run out of vigour, vigour spent, vigour mauled

Lights out vigour, vigour, that is all.

T ragedy has many faces, our news services are brim-full of sad stories. People ask why there is so much misery especially when it involves the innocent. In the world outside of our species we accept that few of those creatures, spawned in millions, ever grow old. We look at how the large attack the small or weak. We shrug, offering only moments of pity. I think we are missing something.

Tangled Twine

Spring

She looked more like a prawn than anything
Still, three feet from an oak tree
Her struggle just begun.
Dead she was, never made a sound
Caught in a half split shell she died
Only saw one dawn.

She seems to have been cheated
Put down before she flew
Her sisters crawled right over her
Left her there, forlorn.
But I saw that poor cicada
On my walk this early morn.

Can you believe that there are television shows about fishing, about all of the gear and the strategies used to outwit and snare fish? To be fair, some anglers return their catch to the water, often with a kiss. It is a Judas kiss. Certainly the fish do not enjoy the sport, snagged in the mouth so that a fisherman can feel good about him or herself.

Perhaps it is time for us to offer other creatures the recognition that being here together and at the same time is one singular cosmic miracle. Perhaps we are not as evolved as we could be. One only hopes there is time enough for us to realise as a species that we might show a bit more sensitivity than we do.

Homo Sapiens
(man, the wise)

'I caught a marlin, six-hour fight, see him hanging there?'
'I swatted flies and stalked a deer, got him in my sights.'
'All I shot was a bag of bunnies caught grazing near the creek.'

'I trapped a fox in my backyard, trying to get the chooks.
But what to do? I did not know, his fear struck eyes met mine
So I sprung the trap and let him out, both of us surprised.'

'You idiot, you fool', one jibed, 'you know what I would do?
I'd crack his head then string him up, a warning to his mates.'

He would.

I could.

You could do it too.

Would you?

The word is out about the Mona Gallery in Hobart. I have tried to catch some of the magic of the walk through an exhibition of war related works. I suggest you list a visit to this place as one of the things worth doing in Tassie.

Art, life and art

Oh Mona, what have you done
You've collected, reflected, infected, projected
Thrown rules out the door

Spy holes, dark places, vents, tunnels and shafts
Things drop from the ceiling, a moment's display
Run to the drains and come back renamed

Coffins and cars, stone boxes and jars
Like a black leathered siren astride her HOG bike
Warping distance and time

Art invades faces wherever they are
Tucked in tight places, it asks who we are
Darkness, air, water, the spark of a globe
Perception is tricky, watch out for the strobe

Embracing the high tech, slapped in the face
Listen and read, vote, take all you can
Today your life changes, you see

Footprints and shadows, loud noise and rude scenes
The senses are tigers, creep, leap, bound and snarl
Emotions, ideas, dreams and machines
Life's got you surrounded, work out who you are.

I showed the earlier version of the poem to my singer/songwriter brother and he suggested we structure a set of lyrics. He then wrote the music and the two work remarkably well together.

Tangled Twine

Coolah
(song lyrics)

What tales this ghost might tell
Leaning, broken, bared, alone
A farmhouse fossil, paddock bound
Frozen in the morning chill

Then Coolah pops up not far off
A cold wind blows and pine trees moan
It pushes at the cenotaph, tracing over lists
Coolah sent its sons for keeps

Grey mist spoons the cenotaph
And it filters through the streets
A traveller stops to read the names
He shivers, not from cold, and weeps

Old farmer stands beside him, silent as the grave
The traveller touches the old man's sleeve
The old man sees the traveller's tears
The young man whispers to him

'Too many Coolah sons slaughtered
Too many gone to war
Sons of Australia taken, fallen
Too much pain for all'

A swelling grips the old man's chest
Sadness turns to pride
The baker and mechanic see it
They cross the street to him

The farmer lifts his eyes, throat humming
It turns into a roar
The town's folk fall in beside him
You could hear their voices sing

'Too many Coolah sons slaughtered
Too many gone to war
Brothers, uncles, cousins gone
Only photographs came home

'Too many sons slaughtered, Coolah
Too many gone to war
Sons of Australia taken, fallen
Too much pain for all

'NO MOOOORE!'

This is for those of you who have connected to pets and have had them in your lives. It is an epitaph for a dog who came to us as a pup, a gift for our daughter's sixteenth birthday from her boyfriend. She was half Doberman, and half Rottweiler, a dog without a down side.

Tyra
2000–2013

I stretch entangled, doona wound
Percolating residue of dreams
The screech of corellas in the park
Slash wildly at the writhing of the day, Tuesday.
There's a gaping hole that grabs at me
A shadow by my side

She rests outside the window now she does
But cannot follow where I go, she does
The back seat of the ute still smells of her
Still half a bucket of dry food waits
Scorched grass is turning green already

The leash we rarely had to use hangs idle
She loved to run unfettered, free
A happy dog and friend to us and all who came to us
Adieu, my friend, but shadow me a while.

Wherever you stop for fuel between Ceduna and Norseman, the big paddock, the Nullarbor, you will find clutches of roadtrains catching breath while their drivers catch up with one another and share the daily news and woes. You have to respect the effort that these people make for the money that is sent home.

Roadtrain driver

Run down critters on the Nullabor Plain
Wonder why I'm driving this rig again
Caught in the spotlight, what can I do
Looking for some way to kill the pain

Don't do it for the money or the lovin' at home
Don't do it for the superannuation
I do it 'cause there's nothing, nothing that's real
I'm another kind of roadkill behind the wheel

I've loved a few women but they didn't stay long
Had a batch of younguns but it all went wrong
So many time zones, don't know when I am
The Nullarbor's the only place I know what I am

Pallets of dog food, got to get to Perth
Don't mind the roos I kill, what are they worth
I'm drivin' right through, the schedule is tight
They're just tarmac mixed grill, I knock out their lights

Don't do it for the money or the lovin' at home
Don't do it for the conversation
I do it 'cause there's nothing, nothing that's real
I'm just another roadkill behind the wheel.

It is a similar scenario as the previous, but from another viewpoint. The question in this one is about the systems we put in place to satisfy corporate needs. Are there any needs other than corporate ones that we might consider? Is everything and everyone always of secondary importance to the needs of big business?

Blood on the wheels

The Nullarbor wind blows hot 'cross the plains
A gift from the great southern ocean
The feathers it stirs, an unfortunate bird
A short life, its body split open

It whips off the bitumen on its way over land
Stirs the carcasses always at hand
Majestic wedge tails, roos and emus
Piled on the verge for the picking

There's blood on the wheels of the roadtrains tonight
Bearing their loads 'cross the nation
Hundreds of tonnes each mountain of steel
And hundreds of critters fall under their wheels
In the wake of their rush to deliver

'It's just wrong' weeps the child, 'why is it so?
Those creatures should not have to die
The trucks are too big, they travel so fast
The price is far too high'

The blood on the wheels sprays into my mind
The child has it right that's for sure
But the convoys of trucks keep on rolling
The toll just keeps on growing

And the child grows into a man.

Sitting on the corner of the big old Queenslander on the outskirts of Gympie where my nipper does many things including write brilliant music, we joined forces to come up with the lyrics of a song that gets the crowds jumping. It does so because it touches the experience that so many of our long-haul drivers have every day.

Highways of lightning
(Camillo brothers 2015)

Chorus
Riding down the highways of lightning
Crackin' thunder snapping at my heels
Lookin' for the woman I've been dreaming
Wondering just how that woman feels

Hard truckin' sometimes leaves you bleeding
Not all the dreams survive the steaming
But I know that when I get to Brisbane
She'll be waiting, happy for the sight of me

Chorus

She's been busy raising all the young uns
Missing all the things she might have been
She stands there watching all the headlights
Waiting for her truckin' man to come

Riding down the highways of lightning
Crackin' thunder snapping at my heels
Aching for the woman I've been dreaming
And I'm wondering
I've been wondering
And I've been wondering how that woman feels.

Tangled Twine

It was the twelfth day of a group tour of New Zealand and we had arrived in Queenstown. It was my second visit and I was keen to test my vivid memories of an outstanding, powerful, intimidating landscape. It did not disappoint. It could also be the twelfth day of creation and things were happening in Queenstown.

On the twelfth day

Great Southern Spirit, sculptor, guardian
She carves and claws and gouges
There's a plan, you cannot see it
But you'll see where she has been

Jagged profiles tear at the sky
She makes her morning pass
Her vapour breath's a trail that softly clings
To ridges' edges, a while, before it fades

She dives silently, unseen, into the crystal lake
And there she rests where glaciers flowed
Her breathing moves the water, lapping at the sides
Her turquoise stirrings keep the water pure

She rests, waits, dreams her art
It all takes shape within her
Tonight she'll carve a river, shape a waterfall
And you will gape in wonder when you see it.

Queenstown

Stark, craggy barren, rising over, they stand
Jagged, ripping edges shaft through the cling cotton shroud
A potent mass to bear down and crash crush
The feeble head spun gaping crowd

The hills, the cliff faces
Always the cliff faces
Ice catch, wet face, stream birth sweet to taste
They let us pass, and timidly, quickly, we pass.

Queenstown tourist town, what's in a name
Bungy jumping, bumpy luging, what's the game
Jump in a jet boat, ride the shark
Traveller extrusion all the same

One sheep, all sheep, cows and deer here
Heads down, arses up, unaware
Starbucks, Ferg burger, KFC
Try something different while you are here.

There is a 'You' in most of our lives, the person who fills your mind tests your very being and rests beside you. Is there something familiar in the observations made here.

Tangled Twine

You

I've been looking through frosted glass, you think
A puddle.
You are puzzled and wonder
Everything's so clear to you

We met
I led
You followed
I followed you everywhere

You were drawn
I was thrilled
It was simple
Neither could know what would happen

Parallel worlds we shared
Our innocence peeled away
War and truce uneasy
Jousting and thrust and parry

Grounded in children you embraced us
Instincts honed across time
Twenty-four hours and seven
And forty-four full time

We did it together
Whatever we did
The rest is forever, together
Together we stand and ever

I thrill to you still, still follow
The fine woman you have come to be
Wife and mother, grandmother
And lifelong partner, a queen.

The Author

It has been said that when you stick your head up, it will get a good kicking. Maybe that is why John Camillo waited so long before sneaking into print in the most unobtrusive way, no fanfare, no big signing or PR program.

His theatre for nearly forty years was the classroom, mostly as a teacher of English. He had moved into TAFE when that subject metamorphosed into Communication Skills. Writing was always an interest, but a painful one because he hated writing cramp. The computer changed all that for him and for his students.

The last ten years of that career were special because his students finally had the tools with which they could learn to love writing. The computer arrived in 1984 at Dandenong TAFE where he worked and he asked his students to use word processing to prepare their papers around a program of activities that made traditional classroom formats obsolete. Their work astounded him. And so, now, he writes.

This anthology is the first of his observations to leak into the public domain, and though it will not make his publisher wealthy the author assures him that it will be followed by more. Anyway, the point of it all is something other than that.

www.ingramcontent.com/pod-product-compliance
Lightning Source LLC
Chambersburg PA
CBHW071359080526
44587CB00017B/3140